THE CLIMBERS

JOHN HART

The CLIMBERS

UNIVERSITY OF PITTSBURGH PRESS

Published by the University of Pittsburgh Press, Pittsburgh, Pa. 15260
Copyright © 1978, John Hart
All rights reserved
Feffer and Simons, Inc., London
Manufactured in the United States of America

Library of Congress Cataloging in Publication Data

Hart, John, 1948–
    The climbers.

    (Pitt poetry series)
    I. Title.
PS3558.A682C54   811'.5'4   78-3753
ISBN 0-8229-3379-9
ISBN 0-8229-5295-5 pbk.

Six of the poems in this book have appeared in *Quanta*.

An excerpt from "Trip Account: Night Climb with Eclipse (Rainier)" appeared
with a mountaineering photo in the 1977 Sierra Club trail calendar. Copyright
1976 John Hart.

"Confrontation" has appeared in two anthologies: *Mark in Time: Portraits
and Poetry — San Francisco* (San Francisco: Glide Publications, 1971) and
Poems One Line and Longer (New York: Gossman, 1973). Copyright 1971
Glide Publications.

To Lawrence Hart
Jeanne McGahey
and Fred Ostrander

CONTENTS

4: Movement by Road

5: Lines Spoken Into a Cave

6: After the Climb

I

The Climbers

TRIP ACCOUNT:
NIGHT CLIMB WITH ECLIPSE (RAINIER)

The sky is the first condition. How it shines. With worlds it shines and we know it and grow shy. Invaders, angels, who walk on their long furred hands — what would they think of our own hands, fabulous under the moon, shaping the rope as for signals to something we cannot see?

We came from the crowded shelter, stall by stall. Where some of them sleep and some of them laugh and others make ready their shoes. The fumes of the stoves were heady . . . how long would the hour not come? There is eclipse on the snowslope. The disk of the shade of our mountain still coppers the light of the moon.

Orange the face of the leaders. Orange the hand. The world discards us and the dream begins. Was it the dream you asked for? Was it a dream at all? When dawn and sleep are equidistant, and the heart stops and resumes, stops and resumes, bent outward without comfort on its valves?

The upper glacier steepens. Behind your back, great dark and three gold domes. The spine observes the lights at Paradise. The blue crevasses. Here one foot goes through. In the flask in the pack, though sheltered from sirens, the water ceases to move. We cannot drink it at the little pass, but stop and tremble and grin.

At the crux we looked for the eyebolt. Sweating, down. Where can there be beyond these holds a way in this black world? Where is the passage of thousands across the invidious stones?

Below us clouds exaggerate the air. From right to left beneath our boots their fall. Under the helmet, under the skull and hair, is a beast lamenting, his little eyes in your own. (You cannot, coward, so easily break the little back of your shadow.) But there's a stranger who'd go forward. Does. And the eyelid cries with light to what it sees.

3

For here there is nothing deathly. Nothing cast, a thousand, into its average. Up in the air, the ice-couloir shines like a jugular. The icefall under us stops in the night, like Jericho after the horn.

I remember the wonderful metals, binding the boot to the hoar. I remember the distance beneath us, very cool. I remember the split-second angel, the axe in my hands. The rock called Gibraltar, smaller now, passing beneath us. And the white slope easing.

— But another light, arrhythmia of dawn, begins to beat its blue across the moon. Till only the bootprint darkens, only the left one. And off to the side you see the gulf: Return. That somewhat, secretly, is feared. To cities never said to be of God. Your dream-like colleagues. Your appalling sky.

Is then this eye, this ship all seamed with winter, very sore, only a thing that the ice made, quick to tear? What was it, after all, we tried? Are we lucky perhaps to find it not called criminal in the towns — or not despised, like pool?

Yes, we laid money there was something meant — prefigured in that night — or frameable. Of toxin sweated out or good begun. Discovered check, revealer of the king. If there was not, and nothing much was meant, we risk the nothing, let the meaning pass. Yet far down under the moon that night, I think the ice was the truth, and the lion's forelock.

In the banal restaurant in Medford, halfway home, your brown companion sits, nor is he changed. But outwards his hands hang now. His eyes without display. For it is his lies were forfeit, his late stars. Brighter than headlamps. Readier even to fail.

And if after strange gods we went, consider: there are no other. I say we have walked on the skin of the Dark Sun. We have walked on the very skin. Let this be an image of heaven — if not this, let heaven be a place more awful still, where gently, gently, into the utter dark, the great walls drop which it were death to love.

4

HUNGRY PACKER LAKE

Below us the canyon opens
like a horse's empty sunlit broken jaw.
Upon the path the print of a foot,
in two parts, like a name.
Upon the stone the scalds of snow,
over the talus,
               into the cirque
that shines like a small cold hand.

Oh lord, our insect, frozen
into the glacier's foot
turn on us now your weeping mantis eye.
Is this your lake scored clean of air?
Your spider hanging like a jar?

Look how the peaks stick up like elbows.
Bony and large
the sun. The trail
stiff like a strap. And we are here
to conceal no more with lip and eyelid
the beautiful stone of the skull.

I put my hand in the water,
drew it out embers.
The fish, bright burrowers,
under the lake's bark rustle,
and would feed.

FLYING INTO LOS ANGELES

This is the costly journey Nerval and the charts foretold.
Which we adore, whose calumnies we bear,
bright as the things of the air are, bold and spoiled.

Under the haze the faint streets shine.
The foul great gimcracks doubling the weight
from which they profit and by which they die.
Do we construe it falsely when we see
among the fires the features of an Eye:
slash fires, burning the fir and the cedar,
false fires, burning the stone?

The ticketed persons mutter, their faces not yet bad.
The lights inform us of falling. The engines change.
And the pilot cries out like a man who wakes up underwater:
"We have won; we arrive; we descend."
Commanded into a three-times-desert land:
desert of earth because of the wind without water,
desert of Man in his stupendous shelter,
desert of fear in the houses of communal laughter
where hope is odious and sought without desire.

— The oil wells. Their wigs of nightmare horses. Their shot eyes.
Their active, clipped, and putrefying wings.
The great unstable sheep of federal towers.
The public places burned or swept by tentacles.
The suck and haul of falsehood every day
into those high black doors.

Do not trouble to ask these roads whom they absolve,
there being none.
Do not trouble to look for the cairns at the exit-cracks,
they being down.

Nor should the hampered and inventive stones,
conjoined in buildings, set apart on graves,
deceive you into thinking: "This is strong."

The guns begin to undertake the air.
From their great mounts the beaten searchlights fall.
For this is a ruin already,
already Guernica.
Deadly it is and out of reach
as the face of a criminal child.

It is by this that we are numbed and slain:
Green shall not be upon this land again.

ELABORATION ON A LINE FROM THE
MANDAEAN LITURGIES

The Mandaeans, a Gnostic sect, rejected all love for this world — the "Tibil" — and thought its Creator both evil and incompetent. They worshiped another, a true, an "alien" God, in charge of Heaven alone. But in one of their liturgies, a worshiper, summoned to that distant Heaven, protests:

"Father, if I come with Thee
Who will be guardian in this wide Tibil?"

Often, Father, have I heard
the story of the alien Word.

And I have memorized the odd
adventure of the alien God.

And I have heard the scholars say
the earth will shrivel up one day

and that the base Creator would
have made it ugly, if he could

and that the sun behind the sky
were brighter to be human by.

But if that insect Archon meant
to make a world thin and bent

He labored hard on his defeat:
No failure ever so complete

in all the levels' history
as that attempt to parody

the Ancient Light in something less:
The parody could only bless.

It may be that our native range
was not this planet, tall and strange

and of such beauty as appalls:
But here our learned allegiance falls.

8

Father, indeed we ask your grace
to shine an image of your face

upon the awful countenance
of rock, and give it lenience

but on the mountain we remain.
I do not think we would regain

your easy splendor, if we could:
The col is bright where Adam stood

to start the errors of the climb
and we have uses yet for time

and beg of you the gentleness
to leave the climbers in distress.

THE ICE BEGINS

The ice begins. The lines of the hills are closer.
Down from the pass the stippled shoulders come.
Already the fluted crystal forms in the spring
like a superior eye.
Already the truth at some of the highest lakes
begins, under furious stars, to be discernible.
Whatever is real in the earth is at perigee now,
the great assassin, but not of the soul,
in the hour before the dawn, when the ice is still,
and no stones fall.

SPLEEN

Against the mountain we require
will there burn a callous fire?

Against the road that we hold good
will serpent spread her perfect hood?

And on the climb that we commence
will falling be the recompense?

To some despair appears astute.
Without precisely having hope

We turn us weeping to the route
and, weeping, climb, as if we thought

Well of the leader, well of the rope
well of the weathers of the slope

Or well of the furious knot.

MOUNT SHASTA IN WINTER

1

At night it shades me. Larger than the screen
on which the kitchen chairs are tall and precisely limned.
Larger than your face. Larger than my own.

On asphalt I walk uncertain. Cannot identify
the substance of my heart. How is it changed?
I think I go more shrewdly into sleep
where always in back of the eye the spun snow stings.
I think I see more often among cars
the slack and perfect features of our wars.
And even on mild streets I wish to know
(such is the howling of the April air)
what isotope is changing to what power.

For I have felt
the cold make entry into my hands and glisten,
axe-hand and rope-hand,
the fingers bent over the blade beginning to sicken
as the objects of the heart grow few and foul —
but look how the eyes get strong, the rays compact and limber,
how the lines on the brain's husk, drawn without knives,
get deeper.

What was put into that cyanotic hand?
What did we buy there? Why
will none of the old reasons clarify
how at that moment all three were the same:
what was given, what was taken, what was desired?

2

Look in the eye and see in the eye behind it
that slope ascending:
how we went up on crampons,
all love for the earth complaining:
the air hauled into the lung like a god out of water,
and the wind, and the slow breathing, and the power.

Far down at the blue joint of the horizon
shine other colors, black, or red, or vile:
But there on white we moved, our shadows whitening.
Even the clear air, brought from the sea to fight us,
was changed to cloud before the face that spoke
of all things desolate and which will not refrain.

Imagine a bird and a sea-thing, bosket of stings,
itself its haven, violent, without effort or desire: so
the surface of the mountain beats with wings.

Remember the lens of ice on the glacier,
cornea of the most unlikely blue,
like some sandblasted, military, and immortal eye . . .
If there is a god, contending with his maps,
employer of hammers to alter the substance of ships,
it is of some such perfect ice as this,
this terrible clear substance, he is joined.

3

I sit in the study, reading the darkened schools.
I cannot even by daylight set aside
the cold companionship of what so much was feared
because you were absent, and the gentle steel
had to make substitute, under my hands, for leaves.

I scrub the windows that disseminate
a little light, as at the bottom of a tube,
onto the desk and the versions, into the blood;
but do not imagine that here, as above in the coomb,
the things that surround one oppose one
enough to make it prudent to go down.

When the mind lies acute, but making no comment,
the five lobes curved in what surgeons call
"the position of function": then the image comes,
shambling, always, like a fountain in a garden,
asking: by what marked? Where sent after? By what thing
impelled to silence under the spider stairs?

I dreamed I saw one walking with a rope
hunched at his shoulder, easy: at his side
his hands had the features of knots: his eyes
had three dark futures which I did not see.

Was it a climber or a hangman that I saw?
— That laughed until the clocks began to strike:
"Who gave *you* leave to fail?
Who told *you,* creature struggling in silver
under the chagrin of my invading eye
you could refuse the entry you descry?"

4

The rock is my template. Standing next to this
Lord grant I not grow vague:
Not move in parlance under the multiplied skeins,
the dreams that, forever extended,
discover us nothing but sleep.

I shall be what I have begun, without disclaimer.

I do not know whether the rock of this place
is chiefly of flesh or of fire.
I do not know whose aqueducts these are,
whose suicides, or whose great voices.
But under my hands today I know I see
such brightness as it were a kind of eye:
and there is strength between us on a line
I can explain by neither stone nor vision.

2

Among the Beasts

CONFRONTATION

The mantis with translucent grin
climbs up the rack of his six awkward limbs.

So on my palm he settles,
vein to colder vein,
stares from a steep face, bony as a stallion's,
at my enormous focus:

the simple and the chambered eye.

WOODS

You say this wood exalts your love:
By that you put yourself above

the place you have in such a place —
rely too much upon your race

to render innocent a spot.
The beasts behind these trees do not

recall or care that you are Man:
This wood will kill you if it can.

AMONG THE BEASTS

Among the beasts the fear began
that they had claimed too much for Man.

For if you took away his knife,
he would begin to doubt his life.

And if you took his boot away,
the earth would lame him in a day.

And if you let his love depart,
beware, what slides within his heart:

a blight malign enough to kill
the thing that dares address his ill.

So let him sit until the end:
the beast the beasts could not befriend

until at last they can demand
his shade intense, immense his hand.

POLEMIC

His shadow grows too large: He overbears
the narrow lands on which his love depends.
Sets out at morning with his guns and snares

to make all beasts his servants or his friends.
O ask him, if the lion's eye should find
him lost among the ruins of his hands:

"Will Man the lord be gentler in his mind
when he has laid the earth before him dead
and having nothing left to leave behind

at last uneasy turns away to read
upon a stone whose speech he learned too late
the lines amended by the lives he led?"

SNAKE

The viper in one long muscle of laurel
relaxed as a lion is.
He shows you one moment only
his long admirable head.

The snake stirs
    like a channel
    to your touch
lifting the skull that's kin of iron
and a simple bone.

LIZARD

The sided creature
pleasant as leather
easy and dry in my palm
lifts with a calf's color toward me

his little and hay-bright eye.

PREDATOR

Under the center of the lake
the images move.
The trout in his sleeve of mica
is lighting the close stones.
And a beast like a surveyor's rod
appearing with the motion of a jaw
steps, and on cold pivots leans.

Fish move and move, more quietly than shoes
from that bright throat, and pale.

THE CURIOUS FEAR

When in a desert valley like old cloth
the daylight hums and thins:
             So on this wind our words
have hung and hoarsened.

And then the curious fear resumes:

That the old tall beasts in their orange barks,
the various, paired or alone, and standing there, may be
the closest things to angels we shall see,
and the panther, the closest to God.

So shape some furious godhead to decry
all vanity not ours.

So set our hot
appalling footprints on the winter sky
and fondle in a high subhuman fist
no further purpose than some war, refought,
with fire, this time,
and a weird and reckoning wrist.

3

The Belayer

CRUCIFIX

Touched the node where six bright vessels bunch,
snapped the blue stalk of a vein:
He felt the blood drawn down his wrist
like a long-stemmed violet fire.

He is dead:
        The ponderous gem of his skull
no longer bears his monumental sight.

The crucifix on the wall-shine
hangs like the curve of a wrestler,
shaken by water its blood has sanctioned.

This is the marred bird of this manor
whose muscles shuddered
around the traversing nail
dissimilar as wings.

NATIVITY

Onto that manger
with a shadow like an owl
a star came flapping.

Behold the chill small animal:
The beast of the delicate thorn.

The star left on her face a wrack of salt,
and she stood there holding a rare flower
like a bane.

\

ADORATION

Into the morning the black star shines,
the stinging arms of its light,
and the flowers turn their small split crowns
on colored swivels after.

The snake already lies on his mark in the dust.
Under the seam of his clean and colored spine
the twelve bones on their thread of sunlight spin.
And a small sea the yellow color of sweat
is sliding on its callouses of stone.

Do you see us, wise men, on leather and outsize knees
kneeling like camels on the alkali,
filling with foam the pockets of our eyes?

Angel, shoulder-bone, shadow upon our lands,
come down, and come alone.
For the knife stirs brightly in its place against the thigh
and the heart stamps on like a foot
and around the eye the tears of rheum and salt
like whips begin to beat.

Is it too late now to turn and run?
About us the smoke of suburbs burns
like a stubble of bitter corn.
In the glass the image of a face asleep
through which the searchlights muttered all night long
is opening its mad colloidal eye.

The dust is distended but no foot comes.
The wind in the yew tree mutters like doves.
Shouldered the branch
but the footprint is empty
that opens its radiant shell.

ON THE RIGHT TRACK

When they began to call it love
a lightning mocked them from above.

When they began to call it peace
a bullet bid the lung to cease.

But when they hung him on the rack
the earth in approbation shook:

There came among them stammerers
to say how right their vision was.

For there's no space where you can move
has not the power to reprove

and there's no image you might love
that well you could be certain of.

So you had better fight to save
the ground confronted by the grave

and with no living creature seek to share
the bitter sustenance of what you are.

CATECHISM

Out of the stagnant font no image shines.
On the white conspicuous altar nothing hums.
But still is glamorous for year on year
the small and bloody exit of His heel.

Those eyes grown wise and fogged with enmity
confound us again from the Cross.
The Host plays back like a piano roll
the palsy and the prey.
"These," they have said, "are the indispensable vestiges.
There are no others on which you dare to feed."
And on the wall the rider is immortal,
His frozen face like a cat's face in the fire.

The enormous nets that swing above the stones —
the strange expanding wharfheads at which ride
the sad-flecked masses of arriving dawn —
what else can *we* make out of Calvary?
. . . The wind in that place a muttering
so desperate, undistinguished, and unclean
that even among the Methodists
their prayer has more to say

When in fell ranks they cry to Him
who sought to enter Heaven as a Son:
And like a climber armed with evil nails
swarmed up the dogwood:
His great head shagged with ice and blood
and helmeted, he told himself, with God.

The intercession that the booth presents:
Will it serve when the snows meet over the ridgepole?
Will it serve when the bright rock breaks?

We look far down:
We do not trust and will not seek to test
the tiny holds the faithful tremble on.

EASTER 1973

Is this the last remembrance of our lord,
his hands grown large with weariness,
going into the darkness as one shorn?

The sky's back broken with azure,
the tree in the water staggering with green:
Out of our footprints the hard lakes buckle and shine.
Under the ground the soft brown muscles of gold
are bunching to throw us forward and uphill.

The angels, lowering their perfect skulls,
more animal than we,
and the great brute lights of flowers,
swinging upon our lines:
                              Though none forgive us,
with luck, as on all winter journeys,
we shall endure the spring:

It is the last remembrance of our lord,
whose hands with vast indifference lie
upon the suburb and the sea.

WALL OF THE MORNING LIGHT

Some would profess their brittleness to God:
These need to fear a closer, brighter stone,
so local are the senses, and so odd.

By photographs we see them: They are shown
upon a rack that has been seen to kill
because the soul, that eye bound up in bone

like a rooster's eye, censorious and still
wants focus on the steep immortal scene
that they encroach on with resolving skill.

The rope that slides across the palm is keen:
Pain is the only error they allow:
But what, on earth, could teach them what they mean

if up above the plowman and the plow
no mountain had its high and hideous brow?

IMITATION OF MacLEISH

Against that time when we shall sit
on porches or on stones, or stand
uneasy where some three roads meet,
foregathered, waiting for the end:

Against that time what words have *you*
made stock of, to put down on stone,
in language that the angel might
destroy with other than disdain?

When one man hung against his cross
ungainly, and in fear, but not
immortal (for the pain grew less)—
Who did not laugh at his defeat?

And should some night have taught us which
commandment, of the ten, was true:
Who were not, who had stood that watch,
by morning, ready to betray?

Until they come, those men grown thin
to set upon the earth their hand
the fearful should at least research
some love they would not wish to end.

THE BELAYER

Among them there is one who shines:
Not the climber who advances,
leaning mortal on his lines
in ill-considered stances

But the belayer who by stone
must make such hazard of his will
that he can stop a falling man
before the fall has room to kill.

Whatever shadow of himself
the climber travels to defeat,
belayer, on his granite shelf,
must have it dead beneath his feet.

And those whose office was to grieve,
the corvid daughters of the air,
did not with greater power weave
their sullen fingers without hair

than he his hands in agentship
that in a moment can become
the butcher's or the gunner's grip
upon the rope whose man is thrown.

For he is set upon a place
where nothing that is feigned can crack
his old and operable grace:
The rope is warm around his back

as if he had in his odd guard
the cordage that sustains the earth
from all erosion, from the hard
and sanguine enemies of birth.

As long as the belayer waits
on weary stone, by duty sane,
the earth by errors or by hates
will navigate to spring again

and this dark rock on which we ride,
this narrowing and subtle land,
is not by martyrs justified
but by the terror of his hand.

4

Movement by Road

NEVADA, SUNRISE

Into the dark like eyes of brine
the headlamps look, their odor of sharp flowers.
The road is northwest, bringing
the color of cross-lit rain:
a curtain that is made to tick and shine.

Brighter, traveler, the clusters of your hand
upon the ancient wheel must burn
than any passing flare of thorn.
For through those tilted palms is light
from dials numbered with small heat
and fixed at Nine for hours.
                              Listen:
the engine drumming
like an altar in its oils.
And still, like a sideways candle,
wakeful the warm eye flames.

Remember those broad flies
cracking their backs on the glass
like a yellow rain:
and lightning, brief and secret glide,
the lizard's lateral hand,
angel, its markings of bird.

You thought among the stones
the fossils stirred like bees:
But see in the mirror still how the eye is wet
with the new shine, cumbersome and clear.

JOURNEY TO A DEATH

1

On a desert written out of salt
the wind goes by without gain.
But in the skull
the yellow stone of the eye is quick
with images. It sees
like veins those roads pass on
that will bring the horse and the rider
through canyons bare of cover
and brilliant as a muscle caught in pain.

2

In valleys where the black rain sleeps
the engine beats like a wing
drawing the traveler deeper
        (O colored oils of his eyelid)
under the roads that branch again like lights,
under the slanting cinders of the air.

3

On the descanting plain
the trees put forth their high invented fires.
Behind Cape Fear the Carolinas burn.
The clock in the suitcase is winding itself like a gun.
And all the stones of the street as darkness falters
rise up with a noise of hooves.

CAPE SOUNION, EASTER

If ever a river went
(color of frogs and noises of digestion)
it went not here
where under the leaves dry day rots back to its stems,
conceals like smoke all faces from the sea
and where alone and sibilant you stand,
your face in the leveled light like a stratified stone,
your hand like a petrified branch
in the branch of your hair.
      And still
some fisherman's sail toward Andros turns,
and the sea to its last black island bends
like the curvature of an eye.
From cracks in the gibbous marble
the goddesses grow stunted and reclined.
All of the boats are gone under
the brass palm of the sea
and temples in the draining light
with all their horizontals gone
subside.

In the trees the beasts are asleep on their brackets.
There is nothing to do but turn
back to the trail, its levels white as a weir,
its joints like the joints of a hand.

Unnatural now the rare birds emigrate
on numb and crescent wings.
The sea beneath them shines like the fray of a fire.
O empty from the ocular

the dregs of the infusion of their light
lest on your eye like the roots of some sick sweat
the odd tears grow
and bitter
dislodge a stone.

ANNUNCIATION

Upon that road the gradient of light
is steeper now. The moon before us
spins to eclipse, its shadow on
the white spheres of your eyes.

Where have you brought us, bird of the boundary stone,
to shine in your piebald noon?
Into the entrance of that land
the shadows follow after,
the clouds turn over us like pages
written with rain
and death that startles like a silver light,

o hawk in the air without foothold.

He covers from the wind the flaws of his eyes.
His face like a small visor does not shine.
And like a hand his heart in darkness closes,
shutting the cold phalanges of its bells.

SNOW BASIN

Should you come to the basin
    where color moves
        like fierce hands in the air

Over the warm-headed beast that is lilac
    and the hard seed of that light blows down
        onto the terrible verges of your eyes

Reverse the shallow heel, then
like a small blind fist:
Turn back the hoof that's lit like a small skull:

Run down each branch and bone of mountain water
    down far from the madden sources
        of pollen and of vein.

MOUNTAIN MEDICINE

"On a coast this cold," the doctor said,
"a wound keeps its shape like a sill,
and death is no spasm, but the faultless moon
conducting, like heat from the hand, the truth away."

You will excuse the manner of his speech:
The wind and the radio garbled the German so much
he could not afford to say much that he did not mean.

Nor run to the window when the sirens start:
Whatever the event we know it brings
to dogs confusion, to the lovers gain,
and courage of conviction to the sad.

RENO BEFORE DAWN

Among the city streets the lights like sores
consult the ancient matter of their pain.
The wedding chapel shuts its bitter doors
and love is on the lovers like a stain.

The lawyer keeps his ghastly hermitage.
The neon burns its circles sere and floral.
To grin upon the cankers of his cage
the gambler pauses in his metal quarrel.

Our dark, encumbered, reasonable ghosts
among these lamps must cringe, evade, or burn
like ships that pass the flaming casual coasts
that all who live do live because they shun.

Across the dull and melancholy stone
a human shadow stumbles and goes down.
And must we leave it, gasping and alone
among the knives and pigments of the town?

No, this is not the place where we have been:
the mountain: on its cold and cabled back:
its rocks that slip: its wrath of oxygen
to break the body if the mind be slack:

Where some hard eye is bright upon the land
to strengthen, on its high dismaying hold,
the climber's lost, his disobedient hand,
and leave him climbing, sentient and cold.

If there is any answer for you here
you have it there already in your pack,
beside the cordage gainly, clean, and clear,
heavy this morning, dragging the shoulder back.

But here's a town for terror. Here the rock
is indeed rotten, and the rope is frayed,
and here it is, not in the bitter cirque,
that the best action is to be afraid.

5

Lines Spoken Into a Cave

DREAM

The tiger crouching, in his eyes
a fire of circumspection;
the smooth-backed soldiers, marching between soldiers,
and the great ships going, their bodies half under the tide: —

There has been light upon us but unnamed.
There has been love between us but unclean.
And the dreamers stir in imprecision,
unable to go forward or awake,
at the hour of the night when there is no impunity . . .

And there that glass
                    (O mutable, o lost)
by which some grace, presented and denied,
was made to give off light and turn away;
to leave you in the morning what you were:
an animal sorrowing under the shack of its hair.

We are figures in a landscape, bent and tried.
It is not the function of the earth to make us free.
Over our skewed maps leaning and afraid
where beat the insomniac rivers
and the insuperable crying of the gulls:
where the lakes of second intensity burn

and pain, bright intellect, through all the hedgerows shines.

LINES SPOKEN INTO A CAVE

Oracle,
speak if you can.
Take words from a guidebook to leaf-shapes,
spread out the white-hot stamens of your hands.

Oracle, rider in the shattered air,
bent back on yourself like the cunning bones of the ear,
was it you who broke the iron-back lizard there?
When the stables were stinging with myrrh
and the horses, sweat of azalea,
shied from those hot wings?

In the gristles of these bushes
a wind stirs, caught on many thorns.
Within the clock like a twelve-fingered hand
the hour clutches at its copper wheels.

Like a wineskin huddled in the rock
the saint, archangel, blue child crying,
usurper at Delphi,
chews at the scars of his bones.

Forever crippled, veteran
of the little war he fought and won,
through whom we know, and huddle near,
our dour and intermediary lord,
remnant of hill and hot azalea,
remnant of wing.

AFTERNOON

In that room a hundred objects mutter on the shelves,
speaking of dreams,
                     of yellow hands of rain,
of broken windows in the tilted light,
of angels whom the glaze of porcelain
forbids to lift and benedict
the bright, the homicidal hand
of anger or of love.

And the bird at the edge of the marsh like a barkless tree
will shake the white light of his leaves.

PULL OUT THE CARDS

Pull out the cards, the small wizard faces
    like the family's dog
        long-headed and blind:

Ask of those eyes, as of the beasts in coral
    the answer that lies already, stinging,

In your mad and quiet hand.

FRAGMENT FOR A SUICIDE

Whatever bird, wingless and cold as a shoe
had been informed
stood on your doorsill saying: Rain —
Was this the angel like an ice-distended flower?

I saw your shadow passing in the rain
as one black-hooded
and at your feet black images of love
came chewing their remnants of wings.

Do their barrows abut on our gardens?
Their names make numb the hot unknotting seeds?

No, the dead like great fish,
drifting under the Bay
grow calmer and calmer
as the systems of the body fall away:

Aware that the dolphins, horses of bitter coral,
have shone among these waters bright as lawns
waiting only for the colors of their room
to reassert themselves and shine
in a pattern of swift hands.

Dwellers in slanted houses, dwellers on piers,
regard the yellow sea considering your stones.
And count the small bones of your table. Hear
what the blue-fretted fish
remarks from the silver pan:
And hear the water clawing in your pipes

like a salt limb of the sea.

MOURNING BY RIVER

Beside us the river,
                     where the artifacts of clarity
ran in the shadows
their inch-deep wheel:
and tears at the line of your eyelid also
began their shunt and sting.

Loosened in the seven quarters of the heart
the black diastole of loss
like belladonna hung
and shone betwen two brilliant valves of pain.

I saw you pick the grievous lilac
       (remember with what weight the fingers turn):
The broken facets of the flower
were exact to mark your palm.

Already we felt the stems of evening air
thrust cold into our hands:

Turning, we heard beside us in the water
light's beast of hooves
and saw shine upward in the pool
its great shorn head
and the clear blind sources
                      of its central eye.

6

After the Climb

ACCIDENT REPORT

The bird is up on his gristle of wing.
Under him granite. The ice like aluminum.
And a climber curved out like a tool.

What jay condemns us to this bright,
                            this barren,
this uplifted shore,
where fear is kindled like
a permutation of our love?
The leader on the glass couloir
who hangs from his steels and glistens
is not than he more shining or more cold.

Go to the climbers.
                Tell them one shall fall.
One on a rope, descending and annoyed
this day may falsely place
his humming, punctual boot.

Like a surgeon who sorts without hope among the veins
I saw him study in the tarn
the floating lines and limits of his skill:
And as the hawk will strike at the meat already killed,
to kill the shadow in it,
so into his floating image there he dropped the stone.

Over these rocks like sleeping faces
the downhill river runs
to salt plains scarified by noon.
The glass bird of adrenalin
shows you his valley here
                       with brightness on
his cold and crumpled eye:
For all these animals are his,

borers, breakers, carvers of his name
on the flesh of the forearm, on the painful
flesh of the thigh . . .

The earth turns and turns in the sling of its winter.
The world has the stance of bitter cold.
The angular flock and pale-headed
crosses the bony weather.
And the dead man still is lying in the snow
his skin bright
and his face, anxious.

INVOCATION

Be with the climber gentle, and correct
the metals that sustain him and protect.

Make chill his eye, perspicuous his route
and more than he his bowline resolute.

Make holds that he can hang on. Do not let
him fumble, scant an anchor, or regret

on granite every fact but that he came:
Make bright his boot and bearable his name.

Be gentle with the climber, and deny
the rumor that the innocent can die

lest on some rude rock wounded he suspend
the awful adumbration of his hand.

I HAVE ONLY SEEN

There are certain summits of a shape so odd
that you could prove the afterlife by them:
ugly as Eiger, having no place on their backs
for a man to stand up even sideways: and lovely,
when lit after dark by the icefall,
as the advancing creatures of the sea.

Nor can be disputed, after the seventh month,
what beauty down the streams begins to move
in a fashion of downhill spawning.
Among red leaves the great death hums,
shaking the ice from his opulent and almond-smelling wings.

By these assured the mourners come, by daylight, early celebrants.
They are so sure that what they search for, found —
the truth about themselves and what they told —
will be their friend.
To a market of great risk they come
to sell the loss which is our home.

Might this not be the greatest of those lies
by which from among the thousand scribbling candidates
the easiest damned are chosen?
They wear bright cloths but under the red cloths
(suggesting bones, the beautiful inside sleeves)
the flames are turbid with their flesh that burns.

— The talk is treaty: I have only seen
the death that no man can set store upon:
a heaven where only the braver-than-I get cured:
where desperate in beauty broods
above the desert and the Word,
that greater, and more cruel, Eiger: God.

       * * *

Once in the stubble of Europe, a bicycle lightless beside me,
the bells of three villages
beset me at once on the plain.
Against the foison of the dawn
a horn was stricken.
In a bright stable of stone the beasts awakened.

Safer to be disciplined to wait
upon the normal stripping of the heart.
Whatever well-meaning, immortal, ancillary power —
whatever it is that over our heads holds the sky out —
the self-healing, insulant fell —

He makes the light that in this room
associates all things.

BOREAL RIDGE

Who can dissuade his hunger? Who so sure
of his seven knots, the tedious, the sere?
The water toughens: in the tarns
the perfection of ice goes forward:
and thin men, cold under canvas, dread
the zero day before dawn

When those by whom their lives were shorn
from alcoves terrible and lit
regard their slow impassioned sleep:
and a thousand go west in cars, and women also,
riding their similar engines, black as balloons.

Nor shall the mountains give these lives an order,
nor the branches of gardens coarsening with green:
On ice the color of iron they shall lie,
by thin lights wounded, by their own eyes destroyed,
who were delirious but saw no road.

And the great lamps cry (for which the rivers were undone)
the dumb and lonely crisis of our will:
"Define it soon: your place is almost gone:
Something up there is being sold for starlight:
And the lovers, who gather for speech in the opera garden,
Are discovered already in pain."

OVERHANGING RAPPEL

This is the death we must endure:
the awful eye of the volunteer
instructing reason to despair
and go down backwards in the air.

This is the order we most fear:
to make a step direct and bare,
to overrule and so to cure
the bitter human cynosure.

And so we hang against the glare
of stars that were not there before:
The human eye shone never here
so brutal, beautiful, or clear.

Assured at last his hand is dour,
safe at the center of his gear,
the climber can return the stare
of rock, and see a likeness there.

NOVEMBER 1977

. . . winter for earth and us,
A forethought of death that we may find ourselves at death
Not helplessly strange to the new conditions.
— W. H. Auden

1

This is the first night of the colder air.

Where the horizon fuses to the field
the long eye misses the defense of leaves:
the glare-ice hardens
over the slope of stars.

And the cold front passes like nightfall
over the stinging town:
a monster of light that suddenly shines and steams.

Dante it was that put
Judas too deep for the flames, in the cold at the center of Hell,
made Heaven temperate as hired rooms,
wherein he placed them all, Italian saints,
forgiven, communal, in numbered spots,
full of beatitude and full of rank,
the image of the false unfading rose.

But I am one
would love to see the glaciers again:
cold heaven striding south upon
the grim and festive dial.

The cold wind, thorning its eyes upon us,
is the slow chill of Eden, coming home.

2

O you who refuse to go south, or to sleep entirely,
or, like a plant, to lie utterly still in the seed —
make no mistake: you are exposed indeed.

Feel adrenalin ride as the storms crowd in —
down through the Water Gap, south into Jersey:

ah, the small blows of the hail that do not mar.

I by this light am shaken out of sleep
as a dog might rattle a bird.
I by this frost am of nostalgia cured:
of the kindly error: ever to think we loved
heaven because it was home.

It is a gentle thing to love the earth:
but never imagine in heaven a better earth,
a warmer house, or a more rapid wagon.

I know my heaven from the impulse of the hail.

3

Believers, Catholic or Gnostic all,
or of those cults
that try to stay clear of the truth by avoiding ritual,
say, while you can, what you will,
while the organ, the wonderful flatterer,
is beating its hail upon hail.

But what will you do, adventure halfway gone,
when the frozen man at last, his hand ethereal,
advances toward you, opening the stars?

What will you do when the soul is left alone —
the last bus departed without you
in foothill town?

And you left standing, under the Matterhorn,
under the deadly face of ice and stone
where the avalanches drag at tremendous bells?

67

4

At the foot of the first more serious slope
they cold and shoddy stand,
the ill-equipped, the quickly trained, whose will
will not sustain them for a morning at a time.

And the rock above is the saint's back. Who will dare
the gold and slotted hide of Yggdrasil?
Desire tilts back the foreground of those eyes.
The gored feet harry the icefall. The twelve thorns.
In their monstrous clothes that appear already to bleed.

But the angels rejoice with harp on copper hammer
the yellow lymph of the primus flaming cold,
the odor of oxygen, rank in the purer air,
and water, its shine of foolscap: its faint day.

And listen: the wolves are coming in their pods
to lick off the last of the dark
from the wakening eyelid.

AFTER THE CLIMB

Alive and tiny at the line of torment
look for a radical tree like a hovel of wire.
Already the stones are fainter, and the air
begins to kill the functioning of blue.

We were the strangest cattle: bawling across the snow
our thick notorious cries:
our great heads hooded, blind at the back, undone:
horns on our boots, our hands
as tortuous as bells.

What is it draws us to these artificial causes,
exposure to height, or to cold, or to dream and dream-creatures,
their foreheads colored like signs?
The street lamps in the night like softened tumors,
under which walked, their shadows shortening,
the thin, immobile moments of our lives:
Are they shining with a light a little less of fever
because the rock sustained us after all?

Our eyes grow smaller and our hands increase.
For each at timberline must pause and turn
from what he was to what below he sees:
feeling the back once more make visible
the weights that it must move:
the harnesses, the guns, the hostile doors.
And now on the bank of the wash that the snowmelt fills
the hot track starts,
down which we shall withdraw
into the other life, where the thousand
bituminous roads and the railroad hiss and shine.

Leaving behind us, over the Shasta Valley,
that siege of ice reared up on bitter fire,
invader of heaven or ghost of it, answering nothing,
and dumb as an intimidating door.

But the travelers in hearses and in cars
refer their faces to it as they pass
and turning the head as the scene turns, lift up those eyes —
the great white filters through which sometimes pass

the least derisive of the holy images.

Shirley Kaufman, *The Floor Keeps Turning*
Shirley Kaufman, *Gold Country*
Abba Kovner, *A Canopy in the Desert: Selected Poems*
Paul-Marie Lapointe, *The Terror of the Snows: Selected Poems*
Larry Levis, *Wrecking Crew*
Jim Lindsey, *In Lieu of Mecca*
Tom Lowenstein, tr., *Eskimo Poems from Canada and Greenland*
Archibald MacLeish, *The Great American Fourth of July Parade*
Peter Meinke, *The Night Train and The Golden Bird*
Judith Minty, *Lake Songs and Other Fears*
James Moore, *The New Body*
Carol Muske, *Camouflage*
Gregory Pape, *Border Crossings*
Thomas Rabbitt, *Exile*
Belle Randall, *101 Different Ways of Playing Solitaire and Other Poems*
Ed Roberson, *Etai-Eken*
Ed Roberson, *When Thy King Is A Boy*
Eugene Ruggles, *The Lifeguard in the Snow*
Dennis Scott, *Uncle Time*
Herbert Scott, *Groceries*
Richard Shelton, *The Bus to Veracruz*
Richard Shelton, *Of All the Dirty Words*
Richard Shelton, *The Tattooed Desert*
Richard Shelton, *You Can't Have Everything*
Gary Soto, *The Elements of San Joaquin*
Gary Soto, *The Tale of Sunlight*
David Steingass, *American Handbook*
David Steingass, *Body Compass*
Tomas Tranströmer, *Windows & Stones: Selected Poems*
Alberta T. Turner, *Learning to Count*
Alberta T. Turner, *Lid and Spoon*
Marc Weber, *48 Small Poems*
David P. Young, *Sweating Out the Winter*